HONEY & SMOKE

SEAN
SINGE
HONE
SMOK

R

Y &

EYEWEAR PUBLISHING

First published in 2015
by Eyewear Publishing Ltd
74 Leith Mansions, Grantully Road
London W9 1LJ
United Kingdom

Typeset with graphic design by Edwin Smet
Author photograph Olivia Seally
Printed in England by TJ International Ltd, Padstow, Cornwall

ISBN 978-1-908998-43-9

*The editor has generally followed American spelling and punctuation
at the author's request.*

*Eyewear wishes to thank Jonathan Wonham for his very generous patronage of our press;
as well as our other patrons and investors who wish to remain anonymous.*

WWW.EYEWEARPUBLISHING.COM

Sean Singer
was born in Mexico in 1974.
His first book *Discography* won the Yale Series
of Younger Poets Prize, selected by W.S.
Merwin, and the Norma Farber First Book
Award from the Poetry Society of America. He
has published two chapbooks with Beard of
Bees Press, *Passport* and *Keep Right on Playing
Through the Mirror Over the Water*. He is the
recipient of a Fellowship from the National
Endowment for the Arts. He has a PhD in
American Studies from Rutgers-Newark.
He lives in New York City.

Table of Contents

Sea

Colored pulp unlocking in sheaves, a black eyelid.
Violet fluid, along an axle of wind, vodka petals.

Moist metallic, windswept curtain branching into roads.
Orange coda with meteor coils, the hands of prism tinfoil.

But we have not finished yet; we can go deeper.
Green gloss, overelaborate, a bandaged lung glimmering.

Embrasure's double bass, folded like charred paper.
Living in an upturned jar, translucent plasma, pink tissue.

Flying on our backs, unbuttoned sheets for dark's dusty pear.
My emerald...remember the bees made honey in the lion's ear.

We Will Never Learn

Where have these disappeared to, the green ones?
Tongues against the darkness are seething.

While ice sifts in your next scotch, poisoned rivers wait.
Cold and clear, the air cut like a cone.

In this dry dissolving, I await you from your glare.
You can see that part of me wants to die,

But you don't want me yet, without moving.
Sexless like an oval, an alien turns his back to you.

Franz Kafka – Serious About Your Safety

Franz Kafka spent part of his day at work making drawings of severed, mangled, and truncated fingers, which documented: industrial conditions, defective apparatus, and malfunctioning machines. The Kingdom of Bohemia is filled with forests and his work focused primarily on the lumber industry. His job provided security, but he could only tolerate it through 'interior emigration,' a trance-like state which permitted him to leave his writing desk. Kafka's room was the 'noise headquarters' of the apartment and when his father Hermann entered the room, the bottom of Hermann's terrycloth bathrobe would rub against the floor. Kafka was restless, suffered from insomnia, and woke up as though he had been 'folded in a nut.'

§

Mountains of Crockery

Kafka's most famous achievement in his lifetime was not writing *Das Schloss* or *Ein Prozess*. It was receiving the gold medal of the American Safety Society in 1911. Kafka won the medal because of his outstanding contributions to workplace safety, and in particular the invention of the modern safety helmet, commonly called a hard hat. Because of his innovation, fewer than 25 people per 1,000 steel workers had been killed in industrial accidents, which was unprecedented.

About his work and recognition, Kafka said: 'You have no idea how busy I am....In my four districts – quite apart from my other work – people tumble off scaffolds and into machines as if they all were drunk, all planks tip over, all embankments collapse, all ladders slip, whatever gets put up comes down, whatever gets put down trips somebody up. And all those young girls in china factories who constantly hurl themselves down whole flights of stairs with mountains of crockery give me a headache.'

Today, the vast majority of workplace safety mishaps are due to a combination of unsafe physical conditions and unsafe acts. Most accidents, however, arise from human error. Statistics show that for every four accidents caused by human error or hazardous conditions, only one is caused by mechanical defects.

§

Robert Frost

Neither human error nor mechanical defects can be held responsible in Robert Frost's 'Out, Out −,' a description of the importance of workplace safety. In the poem, a boy in Vermont using a circular saw cuts his hand off and his heart stops from the shock and blood loss. The trauma of losing his hand caused his death, but Frost also places responsibility for the accident on the saw's hunger for human tissue. Kafka, by contrast, was not personally preoccupied with serious injury. He was constantly worried about hypochondriac illness and endured insomnia, shortness of breath, rheumatism, skin and hair problems, eyesight problems, a slightly deformed toe, an acute sensitivity to noise, and nearly constant exhaustion. His body would itch all over.

Kafka's illness was like a psychological ulcer. His paranoia was a pipeline between his gullet and the outside air, and he was subject to a terrific alienation. In 1911 he wrote: 'In the afternoon my face was so hot and blotched that I was afraid the assistant giving me a haircut, who could see me and my reflected image at the time, would recognize that I had a serious disease. Also the connection between stomach and mouth is partly disturbed, a lid the size of a gulden moves up or down, or stays below from where it exerts an expanding effect of light pressure that spreads upward over my chest.'

Kafka believed to heal himself he had to chew each bite of food more than ten times. His mealtimes were longer than most, and he read at the table. In a 1913 diary entry Kafka wrote: 'I put my left hand inside my trousers while I was reading and felt the lukewarm upper part of my thigh.'

§

The Dark Kammerfrauenzimmer

Kafka's relationships with women undermined his ability to think, but at the same time, they provided an endless source of angst for him, from which he compared people. He saw two categories of people: one category of people understood only details; another category of people understood nothing, but had a inner relationship to Kafka himself, thereby reducing his distractedness and stupidity.

For example, Milena Jesenska, who was born in 1896 when Kafka was 13, made rejection seem like cleansing or purification. She called him 'Frank.' Few or no scraps of sawdust on a factory floor mean fewer slips and falls, and fewer truncated fingers.

Franz (a.k.a. 'Frank'): 'I'm dirty. I always think about being clean.'

Milena: 'I don't think you're dirty, but if you are, I'm sure it comes from your life-producing energy.'

Frank: 'I think the reason I don't want to have sex is because I'm afraid of being unclean! So many squishy noises and juices.'

Milena: 'I think you might hate women. We should spend more time in the flesh...maybe in Vienna.'

Frank did not show up in Vienna. Later –

Milena: 'Are you Jewish?'

Frank: 'We will never live together in the same apartment, not even in the same town.'

Milena: 'That half-hour in bed was to you...a disease of the instincts. You must be an insect.'

Frank: cough...

Milena, to herself: I can still see his suntanned neck. We had been walking all day and he seemed healthy to me. He never even coughed once. I suppose his illness was only a cold.

§

Exploding in Rage Against Every Kind of Human Relationship

It turns out that Kafka's hypochondria was real. He began coughing up blood in August 1917. He died in 1924 of a tubercular infection of the larynx in a nursing home at Kierling, near Vienna. When the cop in *Give It Up!* was like someone who wanted to be left alone with his laughter, all the bits of Kafka's imagination – *the cockchafer larvae, the tavern in the forest*, and *God's masterpieces farting at one another in the bath* – were distilled in the dark winter's light. A picture of his existence appeared to him apropos of this: a useless stake covered with snow and frost, fixed slantwise in the ground. The cop, like the external world – at the top of his esophagus – intensified his hypochondria, but simultaneously and likewise intensified his understandable pride about workplace safety. Kafka made excellent contributions to safety because he was an excellent hypochondriac.

The continuum of his genius does not solely manifest itself in his literature, but in various protective masks, helmets, and

the stupid activities people do that require head plastic.
The Japanese Aluminum Face-Slimming mask apparently
works in 15 minutes and its foil keeps the face warm. The
paintball faceplate has thick pads which minimize bruises
from 300-km-per-hour paintballs; the goggles in the eye-
area withstand blasts from 20 meters. Baseball catchers'
masks incorporate the trusty power of steel wire coated with
rubber. Fencing helmets of dense mesh, like a knight's mail,
are almost bulletproof. Even in Lesotho, a conical shaped hat
made from straw or leaves offers the sanctity and fashionable
sensibility of making its wearer feel safe.

§

The Five Guiding Principles On the Road to Hell

1. 'The worst lies outside the window.' Everything, from
chestnut trees to lint, made Kafka think angels should be
ignored.
2. 'You must possess every girl.' If Kafka saw two women,
one with short black hair and one blonde with indefinite
features and an indefinite smile, he would imagine rats
tearing at him.
3. 'This girl you are not permitted to possess.' Mrs. Klug,
age 26, filled the parlor window with her unbuttoned coat,
and Kafka would like her to twist a knife into his heart.
When he saw a woman dressed in white in the Kinsky Palace
courtyard, he also saw a shadow under the arch of her chest
in spite of the distance. Kafka craned his neck and loathed
himself – he felt this but could not perceive it.
4. 'All comes back to mere needs.' Kafka wanted nuts and
vegetables, not meat. Meat, he said, made him feel like an
alien. He also wanted a fawn-colored velvet jacket and to rest
his head on Milena's half-naked breasts.
5. 'Needs are all.' He could not have all his needs, so he
decided not to have any.

§

Opéra Comique

It was easy for Kafka to get grenadine and seltzer in his nose when he laughed.

§

Plato's Republic

The main thing Kafka gained from Plato was 'the large part the naked body plays in the total impression an individual gives.' Imagine his visible ribcage, the black curly hairs on his sternum like wires, his pointy elbow bones, and a tuft of hair in the small of his back.

§

The Man Who Disappeared

Kafka's *Amerika* was, like Ralph Waldo Emerson's America, a place of self-sufficiency and robust individualism, but it was also mixed with Aesop's myth and fate. Kafka never went to New York, but he imagined the Statue of Liberty holding a sword. He never went to New York because he never got a servant girl pregnant. He never met hustlers, grifters, or impresarios. He never met his Uncle Jakob, who was never a Senator. He never learned ju-jitsu. He was never bilked out of a salami. He never saw 'The Theatre of Oklahoma.' Kafka never felt the cold breath of the mountain streams chilling his face.

§

Regarding the Effect of Such Writing as Jellylike

Between April 1995 and March 2003 eight different types of safety helmets were recalled in Oklahoma because they failed impact testing, including a central impact test, an off-center impact test, a penetration test, an impact test of a safety helmet with minor damage, an impact test of a weather-aged safety helmet, a pulse delay test, and a neck injury test. People wear safety helmets to protect their heads from getting cracked. The prophecy in Kafka's work is that the victim cooperates in his own destruction.

§

'Letter writing is an intercourse with ghosts...'

A folded nut: Breasts: Helmets: An insect's segments. Safety has a roundness and its roundness emerges between the lines which never reach their destination. Only the safety of the nut, the breasts, the helmet, or the segments keep the reader in a position to give a cup to the ghosts, from which they drink.

§

K.

Theoretically there is a perfect possibility of happiness: believing in the indestructible element in oneself and not striving towards it.

§

Ralph Waldo Emerson

A person seldom falls sick but the bystanders are animated with a faint hope that he will die.

§

Aesop

Our insignificance is often the cause of our safety.

Albert Camus

At thirty, a man should have himself well in hand, know the exact number of his defects and qualities…be what he is. And above all accept these things.

At thirty, Augustine described the world as a 'mighty but not infinite sponge' in the immeasurable sea of God. But is there no answer for tuberculosis and the pleural aeronautics weighing down the right hand? Imagine the trenches, the bursting plumes of lemon fire.

Camus did the hucklebuck – not on the *field*, but the *yard*. He was the RUA goalie. Under the geraniums the sand swept with olive heat towards the heated pond, for the grape harvest, which propelled into the wind with purple absorption.

Do not speak. Do not hear. Can you not hear? The mute and the deaf-mute communicate with paralysis, as electricity ceases to flow, as water ceases to pour. We defecate on the landing, but encrapulate ourselves in the room, though there's no heat and the sink is filled with a red sweater like a ballooning heart. Are you fucking listening? I'm eight years old and the only one at home who can read.

After a meal of apricots, sea bream, and mullets, Camus poured a tall glass of anisette, a drink which 'rolled off the tongue like the piss of baby Jesus.'

Wa. Wo. Water. Hater. Words. Worms. Harms. Marne.

Augustine, in 397: I told endless lies to my tutors, my masters, and my parents: all for the love of games, the craving for stage shows, and a restlessness to do what I saw done in these shows.

Camus, in 1959: The little bit of morality I possess I learned on the soccer field and on the stage, which will forever be my two universities.

One of the laws of paleontology is that an animal which must protect itself with thick armor is degenerate. Among the lawns of Oran there is this animal. Protect your animal as if it were yourself, with its concrete pineapple body, among the withered leaves.

From Burley, Virginia and the Orient, the withered leaf is pounded and blended. It is cut, sorted with blades, and homogeneous. The bale of acetate has been envied along the boulevards. The star-shaped filament has fused the air with fire – the crave kind. The paper is fused with food-grade glue. The rip of the match brings fire and the lips bring the breath through the paper.

On momentary acts and long-term projects: Driving to Paris is more of an action than turning the ignition key. Playing soccer is more of an action than kicking the ball. Soccer is the sum total of a number of kicks, puts, throws, and catches. Likewise, *hatred* is the sum total of a number of momentary repugnances for something we hate.

Winds, cars, films, juicy fig women, Berber orthography, quays of the Pont des Arts, chromium-plate cars, *visible keyboard of ribs*, Kabylie Muslims, blood-cough in Mustapha....

The Facel Vega appeared in the second version of *The Killers*, starring Lee Marvin, Angie Dickinson, and Ronald Reagan. Two movie versions were made of Hemingway's short story, one in 1946, and the other in 1964. These films bookend the noir which Camus emulated. So that's what the upturned collar is about.

Obscure information. Who the fuck are you? Humphrey Bogart? Friend of the Berber herdsman? Fuck your gospely windy sermonizing like a piper.

Camus's childhood nicknames: 'mosquito,' 'boche,' or 'short-ass.' Lice flowered in the folds of his djellaba. The teacher whacked him with a ruler nicknamed the 'Barley Sugar.'

The acid smell of seringas and magnolias shaded the foam-rubber ball being swept along its way by a warmly awful wind. The sirocco is a southeast to southwest wind originating in the hot, dry air masses over Algeria, flowing northward into the south-central Mediterranean basin. Unlike its cousin-winds, the bora and the mistral, the sirocco can build gradually over a 36 hour period. It can last for 12 hours and cause 6-9 foot seas. The sirocco occurs in the warm core of a cyclone. It floats over the Gulf of Genoa and draws desert air into its warm center, moving over the Adriatic Sea, decreasing frequency as it moves north.

Fuck you all. I'm leaving your circle. I'm leaving the café. I'm going to buy the *New York Herald Tribune*. Did you see the article on all the gin joints in the world? Interesting nose. Fog tonight on the Zuider Zee. Whatever you say. I'm going anyway.

The Facel Vega (Forge et Ateliers de Construction d'Euro et de Loire) had a Chrysler V8 engine, a top speed of 135 m.p.h., and was produced in France between 1957 and 1961. Approximately 2900 were built – all stylish and fast. The HK500 out-performed the Ferrari 250GT in acceleration 0-60 mph, speed over a one-kilometer distance, and fuel economy. At the time it was claimed to be the fastest production car in the world. Its most remarkable feature were four, rear-hinged doors with no central or 'B' pillar, known as 'suicide doors.' Fewer than 100 Facel Vegas survive.

January 4, 1960: When the plane trees blur by the window their *gnarled surfaces* are not merely plane trees. They're a mechanism in your eye, alighting through the wind like white jet. And the jade among the crowns is that place by which you've come.

As the rage builds and constructs itself along the lines of memory, you feel your foot press on the gas. And the heft of the shift knob moving like a backwards L into fifth gear as the trees make a broom noise through the wind.

There's a place through your rage beyond which you cannot see, and this is the destination. As if a terrific magnet pulled the course of anger from the past till now, so the car twists along the road as the white line becomes a solid track into the horizon which dangles its pit-like eye.

But what the dust means in its language is a middle sea, where you are angry – at the ill world and yourself: *the body's judgment is as good as the mind's, and the body shrinks from annihilation.*

Augustine said: Love, and do what you like.

Italo Svevo

> 'Theory is good, but it doesn't prevent things
> from existing.'
> — Jean-Martin Charcot, as quoted by Freud

No one thinks of submarine paint, but if it has
white lead, turpentine, verdigris, cresylic acid, stearin, arsenic,
      and soluble naphtha
it is a collection of chemicals, the way we, man and woman,
      are vats sloshing with liquids.

Things go wrong in life: a button comes loose and the square
      dancefloor panels
illuminate the violet, spinning boots like flame!
A frivolous moment appears as a velvet backdrop,
which is a door, but it opens into a submarine's darkness.

In Murano, beside the Serenella Lagoon, a workman
lugs a pail, and it swings like a hatless rack, gray as gooseflesh.
Italo Svevo, Mr. Big Seller of these submarine paints:
'I have to stand over them as you stand over a *crème frite*
to see that it doesn't burn.'

Keeping watch on the thermometer, fixated on the factory,
he paces, along the rafters, but a fellow can't be drowsy.
in the dream the factory is a vampire land.

One can taste metal flavor of blood, as it crackles and fills the container.
The irradiated orange synthetics rise like circuitry!

'Who will release me from my machines, so many machines?
I wake up early with ventilators and mixers
and the devil knows what spinning round in my head.
The ventilators blow out what small spark of fire
there is still left within me,

the mixers stir up ugly stuff from my soul
which I would rather forget,
the condensers condense all the fine gasses in my head.'

Inside his head, too, are a complete range of anti-fouling topcoats,
anti-osmosis treatments. Beneath the gray waves, the ripples of sea
wash the impermeable gray paint, hidden beneath the gray world.
To opiate means 'to praise' and the gray world is a vampire-dream.

The drying umbrella in the hallway
clearly represents the disgorged penis
but what does it mean if it's a glove turned inside-out?
We're flying over the ocean, and it's a sphere...
Do you think you can make an end? Us sublunaries
are under the inflated bag, like the gland of a crocodile.

Blood is draining, and we feel submerged.
The moon-mass like whole-flecked vinegar spirals around us
cartoon stars and we step in and go down, dark as pile,
into the gray hotel, holding the rope, clutching one another –
Ralph and grandfather and palomino grapevine, and through
        the portholes
like blood cell rail-yard as we sink, loose-leaf and footfall until ocean.

Until ocean until erasure as clean as can be, with ocelot spots
        and rippling fur.
Until sea salt enters the lungs and nitrogen narcosis as we slant
off into yellow soup and pull of the rope with neon, nitron, and martini.
Ocean me as gold might become liquid and near and rare.

The earth will become a nebula, free of germs and parasites.

Van Gogh Legerdemain

> 'There seems to be no known photograph of van Gogh.
> I find that odd.'
> – Guy Davenport

Niet, nooit, nimmer is the Dutch way of saying no, never, never, and it is exactly what you don't want to hear from your love as you sleep on a straw mat in a straw hut, in Etten. It's 1888: Vincent says: I have tried to express the idea that the café is a place where one can ruin oneself, go mad, or commit a crime. He thinks razors, yellow, crows. Oddly, Theo reports his brother's last words were: '*La tristesse durera toujours,*' the sadness will last forever, and Vincent – saw everything in yellow, and yellow absinthe, yellow corneas, yellow envelopes, foxglove, and tinted narrow stalks, perhaps swallowed paint hollowed with lead – was poisoned? Radiographical examinations show he reused many canvases. He painted things as *they themselves* feel them to be. Hokusai's 'waves are claws and the ship is caught in them, you feel it.' The women washing at the Langlois Bridge at Arles shows a sickening preponderance of yellow, with its dynamite corners and blonde asterisks. Once a blue Zouave asked Vincent what the hell he was doing there and he twisted like a ginger-colored whirlwind and said fuck, I paint them well.

Frequency Hopping

Hedy Lamarr was awarded patent #2,292,387 for her invention, a
radio guiding system for torpedoes which was used in WWII

Windows

Hedy Lamarr climbed out of the window,
& began a pipeline of invention....
Oh, she's my combustible darling
of *Extase*, and silver imagination.

Ions bump into each other in the projector-beam,
in the cellulose state of drowsiness.

Window: map of galaxies, protocol of narrowing worlds,
buttery night, wireless wobble, sleepy little cipher.
Desire via the radio signals: spread-spectrum like dust
floating, but dust that defies jamming.

Player Pianos

Tiny perforations rotating,
like the black uniformed Austrians
in their jackboots and riflebutts. Turn left
to sustain, right to soften. Paper rolls rotate
within their wood container,
directing 'Fig Leaf' by Joplin or 'Sugar' by James P.

Lines are invisible hinges:
their sequences powered
entirely by suction: an auction,
a duck's flute's
touchdown via the pianolist's levers
to musical detonation.

Torpedo

Navy Memo: Hedy's whippen springs a set-off button.
How can we lift her damper or her damper-spoon
to depress a key or provide efficient suction
to her exhauster bellows?

Feel the feet upon her reservoir of treadles.

Pump her return stroke, lower her pressure and, into
the atmosphere, feed the paper into her take-up
spool, where her channel – sealing near the pneumatic,
flexible leather pouch – admits air where her hole
rests against its upper seat.

Gershwin's large diameter rubber hose, her throaty
conductor.

Nude Horseback Riding

The horse's muscular neck shimmies in the stiletto sunrise
as the plane trees drowse under the fat rainy dust.
Her clothes, pinned to a wayward branch, are the vampire
into which the air's blood moves. Hedy, silent as a horse
with its triangular physique and barrel torso rests.
The horse does its stomp of mortared panorama
across the furred field. His chestnut coat licks the wind
like an electric eel. Hedy, airy as coal coated in powder,
swims and mimes herself as a jockey in full silk pantaloons.
The horse splits the air and wind fills its space. The torpedo
whistles through the waves and water enters there
as Germans smoke and dream of *Elementargedanken*.
As the *Zwischenraum* stuffs with air, with water,
the silent region of the film and the silence of the missile
pierces the metal hull with icicle blue eyes. The End.

Freud Knows

'it's choking me.'
– Freud's dream, July 23-24, 1895

Nosebleeds, stomach cramps, depression, excessive masturbation...Emma Eckstein sought Freud's help, who made a diagnosis: nasal reflex neurosis. She had brown hair, almond eyes, and lavender candles. This is known as 'hysteria,' called by all as *'mutterweh'* or 'vapors.'

Freud referred her to his friend Wilhelm Fleiss, who sought to remove the turbinate bone from her nose, to cure her of premenstrual depression, pangs of laughter or weeping. Drainage tube: fetid odor: sticky blood clots: hemorrhaging: flood. 'Patient white, her eyes bulged.'

This is known as 'honeymoon rhinitis,' known to all as sneezing or nasal congestion during sex, or 'erectile tissue in the nose.' He again packed her cavity with gauze, and Freud felt sick; he drank a bottle of water: a small glass of cognac. Walnut-colored liquid in a snifter.

Emma had terrible bleeding for fourteen days. 'She had lost consciousness during the massive hemorrhage.' A big white patch with white-grey scabs: some curly structures. What happened? Fleiss left a piece of gauze inside her nose (enclosed while in the bud). The end tore off.

This is called *'Opfer-Schuldzuweisung,'* known to all as 'blaming the victim.'

Violin (Larry Fine)

Away from the air which is its only
resource, and apart and away

from the Stradivarius door, we know
window means eye of wind.

Here is pale marble, like a flat alabaster ship,
barely there, hearing only its echo, of its inside water.

The dark music by which a violin tunes its pear
reversals, again lights like a square in stone choirs.

The pain goes away
on payday.

Sequence of violins and their dark pegs, rolling
like a victor civilly putting a rubber mouth over his mouth.

There is a silence that will turn: a hammered vitula
actually sparking with upper and lower bouts.

Maybe we're at the junction
where we will not need this anymore.

Yellow spigots and leafy mirrors –
abandoned grain buttresses and pillows of mud.

Devouring our orange holding since the afternoon
everyone's milkweed & mezzotint.

Beetroot powder, ivory territory...
volcanoes may have peaks but a peak is not a volcano.

Some of us aren't even here, some
have happiness mixed in their lilac eyes.

Bruno Schulz

There's never an end for the sea:
Four blue springs screeching on a loam.

Four blood hounds blacked his eye
Not liking his seaworthy ways.

Four ugly little figures
Look into the glass and smile.

The sea's hotel said reap what you sow
Get ready for the ice blue snow.

There's a tattered basket
And four names written in ribbon.

Liquid salmon float in four rivers.
Feed the grains of sugar to a fly.

Living On Nothing But Honey And Smoke

for Albert Ayler (1936–70) & Cleveland

Evergreen leather winterwear and a honky-tonk, but salty glissando,
a man revealing his baby-life in the dark, when the dark was a scattered ambrosia,

but opening plaints with dynamite, and a grill and a tremolo and hard plastic reed.
What is self-evident, he said, was a colored disk, a sword, the cup of indignation.

I have seen the bright wall of the universe, magnified ten times, and eat only green
things. But when President Johnson was a spooky longhorn, the Pope got the message,

a clicking sound with his tongue, the spirit's balafon hymnic, the freak bearing.
As the saxophone wends and balloons, so the vision. It wasn't funny anymore.

Flowering in the very field, his legit sneers, he has sucked the air out of the room,
mesmerized hyena, and brought us back on a kind of ship, afloat & afflatus driftwood...

and the East River took us to the foot of Congress Street Pier where our lungs had dried.
Become Ashtabula, taxonomic, a burned running, a fur peeling, a pure feeling, an orange.

Become an admirer.

Become Olmstead, Parma, and Ashtabula, where translucent quays burn with fox-oil, overweight drivers, gray mosquitoes, a wood flushed with the lashing waves of pine.

Her brunette radar zoned me, gathering buckeye, rucksack, and eyeglass cloth we became river: Ashtabula was the orange wreck of bricks, boards, a nurse.

The mud slung me, part of the forest, to a new river. This isn't tenderness, you know: — it's *worn*. The river, Little Cricket Neck, was burning mineral, iron filing, flies, and tires.

A marvel how rectangular fires make unearned past efforts, so we blazed, filthy nuggets, to the utter gully, wherewith sky like Gethsemane, we sneaked into the guestroom, all cushiony.

At any rate, we were pierced. The clumps of soot hit the windows, all black now, & I exhaled. Become a wizard, a ghost, a spirit, a saint, a bell, a Cleveland, the final cadence, two octaves up.

Become an admirer.

Become Ashtabula or become assiento, the darkness of river, aspergillic breaking into ashunch. Become, yes, admirer.

Ancestors Who Came to New York Harbor From An Extinguished Past

Ellis Island is a little ochre stone
at the bottom of a cloud.

I'm not furrier staring at the fox-colored
sunset. I'm not a women's shoe salesman

going from happiness to unhappiness
and then from unhappiness back to happiness.

Clothed in black wool like black castles
sparks flew off their lapels in a blossoming town.

Think of Jews envying chocolates and cheeses,
their eyes speaking piles of lady's-shoe-heelism

then become worms in an absent city floating
in the inky tea and a silver evening.

On Kazimierz street there's a bar called Singer.
Its sofa pillows, leafy wallpaper, and velvets

remind us that we constantly peer
into fathoms of unfathomednesses.

A slender girl mulberry stockings
has proven that the dead have a homeland

among the arcades. She's a clairvoyant
of human vapor, the grey spine of a penciled world.

Encircle the pillow of grass

> 'There is no solitude greater than a samurai's,
> unless it is that of a tiger in the jungle...perhaps.'
> – Bushido

She shines like wheels
In the orange overcast.

Alone within and the walls
Hover like fronds.

Pulsing with emerald self-mastery
A door slides open.

She's alone without language
As a blade...

A paper lantern and a
Lighter's ornamental pearl.

She's passing and flying
Like a submarine

But the white heaven belly
Means someday baby you'll commune

With daylight's milk.
What do you want me to do?

Whale

In the 19th century, most of the whaling industry was centered around
Nantucket Island, whose population were pacifists. Men would leave
home for whale hunts for a year or more while women would run
the island. In the sperm whale populations they were hunting, male
whales hunt alone several miles deep, while the females remain in
large groups, and run their society.

The light is oceanic green and makes hexagonal
light on the platform with claws and gewgaws of light.

Each side of the monolith forms a point,
and when the moon shines coldly

from the cowl of space (a bell, liquid, as sound expands
and gets thicker in the sea).

Now a sea song
['Amazing Grace', traditional]:

descending like a cork on her waves
floating on her water wall...

Although the darkness made us slaves
to the moon's arresting call.

I could not break from its cold grasp
so bound our paths would be.

Each drifting sound her liquid bell
made us the whale-dense sea.

Each bottle fell to the sailors' bones;
a house on the ocean's floor

And inside her bricks which opened there
I saw a rising velvet door.

A grove of spikes: When the Quaker hunter
espoused nonviolence and stuffed his musket,

sharpened his hook, with its long sisal
and hemp rope, into a puffing heart

bigger than an oat-fed baby, he turned
in the dewlight like a battering ram.

True intoxication gurgled up in a thermos
of adventure. They'd go out for years from Massachusetts.

They were looking,
but their prey were listening.

A sperm whale's ear, bigger
than a fist, hears twofold noises:

the telescopic part hears squawks.
The enlarging cathedral part

hears echolocation —
Squawk: related to the whortleberry.

Correction... a hoarse squall, never from a horse.
Sometimes known as night heron, with a creak,

a screech, a ghost eating caviar.
Utter like a public-address system,

like a bimaculated duck, with windup gears.
Next to the inflatable balloons, there's the echolocation.

(See under: bat versus manmade devices)
Radio signals sent and reflected back,

from the altimeter to the moth. (See under:
torpedo guidance, silent films, Buster Keaton doing marimba).

Concealed in space: male spermaceti whales
dive 3,936 feet. Females dive to at least 3,280 feet.

They dive for over an hour. Squid beaks are inside
the stomachs. Picture a gray rose bigger

than a transcendentalist's room up in the eaves, like a matrix
echoing its math-maze of osmotics.

Dr. Johnson, in the 1755 Dictionary:
A <u>network</u> *is any thing reticulated or decussated,*

at equal distances, with interstices
between the intersections.

That's why the image of wooden networks
banging a reggae less a private ventricle

than sound immemorial to the order of air
is a membrane gliding like soapstone

to bodies minced which has sixty times' air's
intensity! All underwater: a blue ghost

sucking the fieldfare of smoke: Blueaproned, bluetrampled, bluemantled,
and blueglimmering home.

Jaw bones in an arch: When the whales eat,
they eat in a herd's harem. A solitary bull

joins a school of 10-40 adult females
plus their calves, the length of a breeding season.

But the big squid are smoothed red
lengthwise-jettisoned like a jet,

which, wholly isolated in dark, has pink saucers
and terraqueous chitin, but don't bite

the minute semitransparent threshing of flesh
mounting the portico of its mouth inside her mouth.

Sperm whale uses his head's oily buoyancy
with his bloodflow, turning the oil to wax

convulsing dried blurred ink
to a snowy chamber, extracting air between globules.

When I die I want to feel like jumping
through the keyhole in your door –

[nitrogen narcosis] and be sent in a single infatuation
to the sea. Because I have my own 'transidiomatic affinities.'

The female leads herself into dark
realities of whale moments, intermitting between

her occupation of calf-care, in the Sargasso's alcove,
fastening her hearing

to the echoes' vault. The male hears it
and resurfaces,

saturated with squid-ink, refusing the evidence
of tiny holy eyes,

melting clerical burnished flames,
at the rim of each echo.

Savage disorder when we enter nature:
the gate creaks among the weeds,

we forget why we've come to begin with
and with a downward glance the muscles

in our necks tighten as if a blood-red ribbon
has been tied to the oaken door.

It is a door which restricts entry –
interior predetermination – and eyes

the mass of the next room,
where the speechless, unspeakable

echoes rest, in the vast, interspaced code.
[Reprise. 'Amazing Grace' coda]:

the sonic waves from a mother whale
travel through the oceans' space.

Each darkening sound of metallic hail
receives amazing grace.

Light: skin's desert fragment torn
where there's a fist

where skin is a whisper, whenever
the moon makes its dim

sink in the lake's basin: a train's
stiff haul in the night.

Light: lemon pinwheel, when the rind
waxes a flittery forced timesheet

that's torn then punched, making a cannon
filled with iron pill.

When it's swallowed they fly
like a yellow eel and smoke rings it.

Soap: removing its surface from itself,
with bubbles like a cauldron,

the air moves away from it
in spheres composed of a shine

driven in fabric swirling like a window
approaches to a jump, and bursts.

Soap: not a filth magnet, to get through,
like a cupboard's color,

reversing its convulsive prefabricated texture,
this brick closes around its pores

with its wire stairs and brushes.
Perfume: even though we live in an amber-solid whorl,

we breathe that floating mechanism
by which amber unlocks its petals

and fauna, dancing as a tinge
upon the resin in its document.

Perfume: a coloratura askew like a cascade
within a spotlight makes impending change when she is rubbed: 39

notably electric, along the Baltic shores,
entombed in aloe-wood.

All its life a river mimics the sea,
the one with the upturned moonrise,

and is an instrument calling washable smells,
and light, and clean bricks pouring velvet

incapable of trembling.
Head: beyond the blanket scaffolding

is the massive pulpy anvil. Etched in barnacles
is the steam engine script from an ancient language,

Macrocephalus of the Long Words,
which is its name.

Used for light, soap, and perfume,
its oil moves like foam.

Head: a cathedral, I have said, and a pulpy ghost,
white as a stiletto, and within its coils

are energies which harden, and glitter and palpitate.
In lampshade lace and photographic liquid,

its group song
pleats tiger trim, swell satin, pink ash,

feathery chenille surround, and felt velvet
and it eases as the water table tilts, dimensional.

'Humped herds of buffalo by tens of thousands:'
whales are the humans banished to the sea.

They emit their undersea and trans-watery signals
with their thoughts

larger than a bus, which is like communicating
through telepathy.

Evil walking at midnight: a low, harboring call
meaning to get away from a ship.

Bell shines like: a hull painted green...well,
don't hang around. Don't want you hanging around.

Ice sled sinking: I take the waves by the reins
and am an accident waiting to happen when my weight follows.

Scooping the clam: our troubles are over
when dry land tempts with its crow call.

Introspective strum: Whales
move in darkness,

and in its blanket of cold
their head wax hardens and liquefies

like the manufacture of pianos, with 18 rock-hard
inner and outer maple rims pressed and wrestled

with amplified soundboard into a shapely dome.
There is sound in the open sea.

The complex motions of whale wax
within the globules in the whale head

transmit and surround the front and back
as a soundboard in space and move through water

like a grave carved from the graphite drums
registered within our ears of pillbox size or smaller.

Whale ear, ensconced in bony
auditory bulla and connected with tissue-drawn

sound to the jawbone and its cavalcade to the brain
is vaster than everyone we love.

Its curling organ is the drum itself —
massive tympanic bone, cradling the instructive twofold

inner ossicles called malleus and incus.
Like the instrumentalist's revolving vane,

their involucrum opens with vibrato, with its spinning
motor ascending from f like a yarn-wound yawn,

it is sustained and heard. A boat in front of this sound
will crack, disperse, and become an only orphan in the dark.

It is not well known how boat-barnacle-stripping chemicals
cause deafness in whales: when they do not receive

echoes, as in the blue-black caverns of their planet,
they beach themselves. When the enormous fatty structure

washed onto Chilean sands, it was an unknown organ,
though its skin no longer covered the tympani

and drumrolls of that oratorio many miles down.
Like a man whose hands are handcuffed to his steering wheel,

disruptions of their elastic ligament and synostosis,
make them deaf hulls: the air-filled rotational axis

is unplugged, the stage goes blank, the cellulose
in the film bubbles and burns.

Music encoded in perforations:
In the lacquered, electroplated positives

known as the mother of early grooved masters
there are limited numbers of discs that can be made.

The stamper wears out. The pressing breaks
into a shard.

What is beneath the normal levels which subside and surface
over moving ridges and troughs, between one

and the next as undulation, livelier than breath?
Where should we go on the convex of land,

between the hollows, where the rounded snow
of water reduces itself from the wind's action,

and we're alone beside the leviathan, as phenomenon?
Under the cyma or ogee molding of the great arch,

not of whalebone or cathedral carving,
but the universal, zigzag ornament of waves?

These are the rhythmic alternations of disturbance
and recovery, like sound, like light, like perfume,

with particles transmitted like messages in the air.
Along the nerve we move restlessly.

Scott Joplin

1

Son of a slave, your birthday is no more exact than a petal. Sun Flower, you have no need to worry.

Your piano rolls have played in middle- and upper-class homes. Maple Leaf, across the plains, where it is gold, we worry.

You neither improvise nor play 'blues' but compose. Chrysanthemum, our ways of living differ, like worry.

The weaponized, invisible boundaries of America keep you. Eugenia, there is a reason to worry.

You were composing, but not recording. Only rolls with holes. Lily Queen, others have been pieces of worry.

The reason you asked, and the reason I don't have the answer, is the same. Heliotrope, let's just not worry.

Syphilis, with its attendant dementia, paranoia, and paralysis…Pineapple, your leaves each veer and heave towards worry.

2

Piano is a hammer with action: in other words, the sounds produced when the strings are distinguished. The harpsichord and the spinet, plucked of their wrought wires, are unlike this Klaviatur originally limited to pianoforte then the modern upright. Bartolomeo Cristofori, hammering his gravicembalo as Florence turned in the dusky mode into dusty notes. Between one and three strings per note, that is. These strings are strung to their tension. I myself am strung between 180 and 200 pounds in a frame, though not of iron. Covered with felt, I 'feel' my pedals, sustaining and dampering…allowing me to continue to sound even after I (my keys) am no longer depressed. My 'soft' felt produces quiet. Notice my compass in excess of seven octaves. My lyra. My resonanzboden. My Gehäuse.

3

The Legba Vévé, or graphical invocation: Guardian of the Crossroads

Folk dance: In the Yoruba pantheon of Benin, Legba's a trickster gatekeeper

The New Orleans brass bands weren't screaming 'Les Bas': it was always Legba

To worry = to blur: transgression = the crossing of a line

Ornamental floral patterns: Be aware of its camouflage, which is subversive

Schmattezeit: Ragtime

45

4

All the magic: bristle-topaz. Vine-smoke. Rust. Chalkboard. Apricot glaze. Niue, Montserrat, Palmyra.

Sky's grey crystal. A bridge's bizarre design.

Do You Believe We Shall Know Each Other When We Meet?

a black balloon, that your breath keeps and measures

These are sweet woods and long-loud shouts.
How the still voice is calling, and how people are listening.
What shall they call us? They could call us Married.

They know of a shuttle swift
And of a fairy gift.
We have such *abundance* while *you* perish with hunger.

Tensions in the knot outpace the geese
As wrecks sink to the bottom of everywhere.
You dispense your sheeted snow

And take my ocean to your shore of low
Low-hanging sentences — bent as a gaze upon the thrifty sunbelt.
And a few nickel cat furs rest where our pillow is ours —

I love the windowpanes in the sleek clarity of haze.
Praise all the gardens, radios, diners, guardrails, and hail.
You reach my cord

And let in, as usual, with exclamations
The delicacies of my flex and bow.
I'm an orange shadow...

Enshrine my dissonance among your peaches.
I'm going to sing this song.
I'm not going to sing anymore.

I'm an orangutan trying to play the violin.

Eating in Silence

Anger is a pulse whose clattering
is inside the glass heart and the gray cathedral.

Slice the peach through the plush mantle
into the wiry devil's den. It is her splendor.

The woman next to me won't sleep with me
and the woman I want is in Romania.

The Danube's blue architecture haunts
the bears' dreams; they dream of blueberries.

Do not resist the rage; instead, face into
its burled finials and artichoke fringes.

Food rests through the taste buds,
where it wakes to the thunder of collapsed ideas.

Hunger, that unwanted weather, soaks
the outer fabric but leaves the skin dry as a pelt.

I reach into the fog to touch your shoulder –
the blade and its rose whispers cut the air.

The riddle does not exist...
See the solution in the vanishing of the problem.

Crusty bread, the consonant between vowels
of butter, coaxed among cloud cover of a spring day.

No one can guess the time from the raisin-colored light.
He drones like hot magic. She is cradled by night root ground.

Tongue against reed, dear constancy, tongue against tongue.
Romania is a distant place, powdered with snow and the lost name.

Put On All the Lights

Three of the R&B singers took refuge in the darkest plush of Bamako nightclub. A sound erupted between them. Here the velveteen memory grows weak, so I don't know if it was a fight or a wakeup call. But I can still see one of the women they had abandoned, standing by the bar, with its ochre padding and brass pins, yelping like a ragga, her hair thrust out like a pool, fighting for supremacy. Her ping-like crystal yells proclaimed above the fizzling light...Was she a victim? I have no idea. The gods of noise – her sisters – had condemned her to the backwoods of AM; but the chandelier above her head, hailed its beams like dust upon her head.

Treatise on Hank Mobley

Mobley talked about revolution.
Asterisk, palladium, forever unjaded.

He talked about two lives – the one we learn with
and the one we live after that.

Mobley slowly moped,
as if he was impersonating himself

in order to annihilate it.
Mobley referred explicitly to everyday life,

'I put my heavy form on them, then I can
do everything I want to do.'

Think of Leeuwenhoek,
smaller and upside-down

through his own lens,
to capture the place as a sound,

yet in making that sound,
tightened the grasp on the material

that supported his question.
Mobley talked about what is subversive about love.

When the door to a room closes,
the light, orange as a feather, under.

Mobley was positive about the refusal of constraints.
Strung out, his rung in the ladder broke, as

anyone who can swing can get a message across —
People who talk about revolutions

and <u>not</u> these things
have corpses in their mouths.

Black Swan

'sunt lacrimae rerum et mentem mortalia tangunt.'
—Virgil, *Aeneid* I, line 462

1

These are tears for events and mortal things.

2

Newark, Penn Station: A man tries to decipher the smudged indigo ink on a train ticket, which shows the point of origin and the destination. The ticket is only good for another hour.

Another man is begging for a break and says he's just been released from jail: could he have a coin, a plum, Night Train, nitrous, a ticket out of here? One man is too preoccupied to wonder and another is moving back, away, and shuffles blankly like a slab.

Was he really in jail? Was that a splint? The beef-colored plinth on which he's standing is blotted with black dots, old gum, where the train will come. What is in his bag? A man, black, asks questions of need. Need, a node throbbing beneath the transparent sheet that is the platform's air, is a dangerous deed: he seeks a donation to the '*Rufus (Swung his face at last to the wind, then his neck snapped) Fund*'. Centuries of pylons, elaborate collars with rising forked bells, quick grits with butter, all horrible stanchions seen from within the field, yellow like a crop, but beaten around his eyes is the inevitable truth: I need a ticket, spare a dime, a ticket out of here.

Dreadful Machinery

The Cygnus atratus, or black swan, is sometimes a 'cob' (male) or a 'pen' (female) and in groups a 'bank' (on the ground) or a 'wedge' (in the air), a literary symbol even before their discovery in Australia. It has also been the name for any *high-impact, hard-to-predict, and rare event*.

Look into the night sky, focus on the textured grain within it, where the feathers part, and the motor hums in the labyrinth of the muscles' stricture. The bird-brain with its geographic locator spots the places where the coal burns not extinguishing. Who lit the fire there or was it already smoldering when the blue lights and red lights shined upon it, like a map that was wrong? The territory is dusted with black.

4

How to explore the effect of the Newark riots? How do the city police escalate violence? How do the state police escalate violence? How does the National Guard escalate violence? How do female looters strip mannequins? Does Anthony Imperiale hate blacks? Does Amiri Baraka hate Jews? Does Amiri Baraka hate whites? What is Black Power? What is a liberal integrationist tradition? What is everyday folk? What is a city peopled and run by African Americans? What is deindustrialization? What is white flight? What does it mean to listen? How do you weigh the split city? Where is the music? Unscrew the bulb and feel the darkness reaching for your throat.

'The door's pneumatic snap'

The history of Newark is central to understanding the political narrative of race and Civil Rights, and the story of this political history was largely ignored, even though there exists substantial evidence in the *Newark Herald* and the *New Jersey Afro-American* from ordinary citizens writing letters to the editor that described the caste system and forms of protest against it.

Jim Crow, that other gun-slinging bird, was not isolated in the Southern states, where it was visible, but had a red beak and leathery acne-red wattle in the social fabric of Northern cities like Newark.

6

Hockshop, tourniquet, verdigris, spillage of weight, a city... each veined leaf, the veined neck, yellow like marble, a boarded department store, dime store, dime bag, middle gap between red lights and blue lights, a police horse's breath. Riding across the yellow line, it is a divider, the division symbol, less and less remaining. Flaxen and flexing the light distilled like vinegar & shame, it is a place wrought from bricks solid like amber, and the insect stuck within — its angles — knows not what happens to it.

Antennae cocked and attuned, she once whispered among the passages between winter and spring. Places seeking bus fare out of here, like St. Louis with its elms, Newark with its yellow elms, Newark's backdoor covered with a curtain: empty grape drink bottle, upturned ribs of an umbrella, prosthetic leg, beige with emptiness, a plastic ruby, pamphlet on Esau, detritus.

7

Newark is a model for ways a democratic process can breathe new life into a place terribly wounded by riots, racial conflict, and military intervention. Reject the principles of segregation and isolation: commit to a public culture. Recast the categorization of 'urban crisis' as the central theme of historiography on this topic to reemphasize the resiliency, creativity, and productivity of black political culture to fight against Jim Crow.

Kazuo Ohno

The question we all need to ask ourselves is: Are we genuinely free when crammed into a sack? You there, your eyes are filled with longing. What are you seeking after? And yet, the freedom you enjoy while crammed into a sack is by far greater than that you'd have without one. For all you know, my body could be a sack.

9

Similarly, African Americans used innovative tactics in Newark to gain political power: self-help organizations, court cases, and the electoral process of municipal office as being powerful responses which were unfortunately, or even tragically, compromised in response to feathery white backlash. Sometimes the same liberal-minded people who stressed racial equality were so disillusioned by racism that they embraced nationalism and separatism. Baraka's father was an elevator operator at Bamberger's.

Down, Down, Down

Newark was New Ark when it was new. Now, Newark is a new walk to a New Ark. Newark and new and work and new and work and work anew. Work and new and work and working and New Ark and two by two. Newark and new and few and work and walk and Newark and new and renew. What does Newark, then New Ark, talk about? What is the talk of Newark? Newark renews.

II

Gender intersects with both the operation of racism and with acts of resistance. Because both women and blacks were excluded from the public sphere, they sought civic power through the pieces of public sphere left to them. Despite black power's inclusion of various viewpoints and constituencies, by the 1970s Black Nationalism eroded public debate because of its adherence to racial purity.

Gin and Wine

Newark, n. – A city of northeast New Jersey on Newark Bay, an inlet of the Atlantic Ocean, opposite Jersey City and west of New York City. It was settled by Puritans in 1666 and is today a heavily industrialized port of entry. Population: 281,000.

Double V

African American civic activism was encouraged by Jewish grassroots protest against German businesses in Newark's Central Ward, where publicity from *The Jewish Chronicle* focused Jewish residents who marched, picketed, and boycotted German products. Similarly, African Americans responded to the fight against Nazi Germany in ways that laid ground for a rising political consciousness in Newark. The 'Double V' campaign, a term coined by a Cessna Aircraft Corporation cafeteria worker in a letter to the editor, described a connection between victory against fascism abroad as a goal tantamount to victory against white supremacy at home.

This dynamic movement was connected to the expanse of a rising print culture among African Americans. By the end of the war, estimates show that four million black citizens read the weekly newspaper, and their illiteracy rates were less than half those of white immigrants. Papers: money, rolling paper for cigarettes, verifying identity, a document.

Pier Paolo Pasolini

Photography is the extreme effort of the witness who tries to remember the detail of an action which he has witnessed without participating in it. It is, then, through the imagination that we engrave the photograph with what it lacks, that is, movement.

Helen Stummer

Any explanation of what my work is about, what I am doing, or why I am mostly compelled to communicate the struggles of people in despair, is elusive. Each time I think I find an answer and begin to write about the connection within me, the answer changes.

16

There was a tense dynamic between the potential of interracial activism and its limitations. These limitations ironically became more fortified in some cases *after* the 1963 March on Washington: certain members of CORE and SNCC began to experience rifts as rhetoric from black nationalists alienated integrationists. *Curfew* means 'peasants who cover fire at a fixed time to prevent a larger spread.' The complex and fraught history of these rifts intensified the dramatic tragedy of July 12, 1967, when John DeSimone and Vito Pontrelli, two police officers, attacked John Smith, a black taxi driver.

Jeanne Lee

People who talk about revolution and class struggle without referring explicitly to everyday life, without understanding what is subversive about love, and positive about the refusal of constraints, have corpses in their mouths.

A Nation of Two Separate, but Unequal Black and White Worlds

A mimeographed copy of instructions shows how to make a Molotov cocktail. News coverage (from the Rainbow Peacock, NBC) rarely showed the extent of police brutality against female protesters. Related to this Russian explosives issue, comparative studies show news coverage here and in Russia were vastly different. American coverage found whites as victims, while Russian coverage depicted the riots as a military conspiracy to quash repression.

What Is Lost, What Remains

I've changed.

20

There was a thin lattice of irony in not only the reaction to the riots, but in the riots' consequences as well: for example, Baraka's demagogic sexism, homophobia, and anti-Semitism, taken for granted in many militant reactions. Klein's and Bamberger's department stores were open. Female mannequins, the maquillage of smooth, were twisted apart.

George Oppen

There are situations which cannot honorably be met by art. Some ideas are not politically useful, or useful to the childhood of a daughter.

Walter Benjamin

To articulate the past historically does not mean to recognize it 'the way it really was.' It means to seize hold of a memory as it flashes up at a moment of danger.

23

Poetry pursues an inventive way of describing the interlocking meanings of decay in Newark. We should care about poems because they not only illustrate intensity. Poems illustrate something else that empathic inquiry can start with one idea: to look at cities, and then ask one's own mind: what else have you got to say about reading cities with love?

Don't Stop, Don't Slow Down

Household items such as tar, strips of tires, sugar, animal blood, egg whites, motor oil, rubber cement, and dish soap can be added as a thickening agent to help the Molotov cocktail burn, to make dense smoke, and to help the liquid to adhere to the target.

25

Poetry helps us to read nuance and subtlety into 'urban crisis' because it does not take politics as a way out, it constantly refreshes and engages language, and it engages the reader not as mere consumer, but as a producer of the text. Therefore, the reader's ethical and imaginative sensibilities are employed with the mechanisms of a poem.

George Herbert Mead

History is always the interpretation of the present.

27

With the increase in credit cards and purchasing accounts for shoppers, African American women in cities across the nation protested discrimination in lending, inflated interest and terms, price gouging in the poor neighborhoods, and inferior merchandise.

Amiri Baraka

One of the most baffling things about America is that despite its essentially vile profile, so much beauty continues to exist here.

To Press:

Newark, a zipper unlocking, reveals a headless amulet with an eye, perhaps the rheumy eye of a corpse. Above the cloud-shaped presses leaving leaflets among the yellow twigs. *To Press* means: a throng, affray, to undertake, weight-lifting, or in basketball, close marking by the defense. An instrument, toggle & cam, the media. It imprints the surface, smooth as yellow wine, it is the middle of oppression.

Hence, *press the flesh*, expression, the apparatus to extract juice like cider. The way Argentina means 'silver,' this city is really an Ark, of so many cubits. Tormented as they are by rising floodwater, a music built of bone, sidles along two by two, known enough, meeting under the canopy again, with a new body, a four-digit pin number, hollow eyes, & yellow coils.

30

Life magazine shows the white mannequins unscrewed by black women; the trunk has a kind of pinion that, turned to the left, unloosens. The plastic white legs splay this way, then the jug-like trunk with their champagne feet. Each limb sticks out, or up, in the monolith's cascade. Black women deliberately disrobed the mannequins, since they obviously didn't represent the constituency of the stores. All mannequins were naked. A body holds a sack of households goods (not liquor), and another body – plastic – is in a sack. The word 'soul' is spray painted in black on a window.

Suspect #2

'Black male, dark complexion, approximately 5'8' tall, thin build, early 20's in age, a moustache and side burns, clean shaven chin, wearing a dark leather jacket, a black knit cap, and a green and brown shirt under the jacket. This suspect possessed the handgun.'

Paul Valéry

The mere notion of photography, when we introduce it into

our meditation on the genesis of historical knowledge and its true value, suggests this simple question: Could such and such a fact, as it is narrated have been photographed?

No Easy Walk, photographs of Newark

Cinder block, cracked branch, broken brick, paper puddle, mud clump, mangled chainlink, lace curtain, ripple field, shower rod, shadow dance, tea stain, tinsel light, junking money, freezing day, squirrel tangle, flipping nasty, dirt banks, glass debris, rotted banister, mouth shut, food stamps, viewfinder, no loitering: in the Central Ward where she lived all fragments were rotting in the soil, and below, the rumble was a question.

Diane Arbus

Most people go through life dreading they'll have a traumatic experience. Freaks were born with their trauma. They've already passed their test in life. They're aristocrats.

Alfred Lichtwark

No work of art nowadays is so carefully studied as photographs that depict oneself, close relatives and friends, a lover...

36

Imagination is the connection-making aspect of human intelligence, and poetry allows for multiple, conflicting emotions to coexist. It describes that of what we have been unconscious, while preventing erasure of those fresh sense impressions. Poems last as beautiful art objects, but more than that, they decrease normalized indifference and state the poet's values, her general affection for cities, and her intention to tell the reader: an empathic reading of cities cannot be corrupt. We should care about poems because they ward off not only outside messages of defeat, but also those within our own at times shallow selves; artistic inquiry into urban problems will yield fresh answers.

Old Vaudeville Joke

Newark is the place where the Pullman porter comes in to brush you off for New York.

D.W. Winnicott

In the artist of all kinds, one can detect an inherent dilemma which belongs to the co-existence of two trends, the urgent need to communicate and the still more urgent need not to be found.

Hannah Arendt

One can resist only in the terms of the identity that is under attack.

40

Newark renews after, even wracked forty years after, renews, and soldiers. Newark reneges and soothes. Newark renews.

Underworld: to rub and scrape. To make new, or as new, again; return. Herbs to renew, old temples. Purged and enchanted. New dye. New wool, new tool, look; the ladle and spoon, the nerve, the green and golden. Fresh ice cubes. The visceral plane must be renewed. I'm waiting for you to turn me on.

Newark woos and can lose. Newark works to renew. When viewed, the news in Newark is new shoes. Move and tune-in to the stove: the coils heat and reveal the rune: Newark renews.

Poem

Knowing your shoreline
      its auburn thirst

creatures inside sing
      one has black hair

our legs gnarled
      behind the mirror

raging with a mountain of birds
      the song plays

but now the bloodhound
      of your heart starves

and wants to get married
      and buy appliances

as the world unto our home
      spreads our grease our pudding

to red hills where loss is

•

There are few scars
      a slight tremor

a Chinese girl taken out to the forest
      who thought she saw God in the exhaust

it is the full gallop of foam
      fallen like a cake

but it is her — half eaten
        as a man peels off green gloves

meanwhile a woman opens
        zinnias with full pods sucking

the springhead of muscles

•

Your heat is a shape of a fish —
        pulpy and ecclesiastical

faint hairs on the shape
        like a chain the color of soap

I watched you
        take off your shirt

there is a seed in you
        olive of light

sucking the edges
        in the throes of your magenta

I woke from a long thing
        sleeping smell

and you thin as a bean
        said my nipples

saucers spilling dark —

Ken Burns

> 'There's no such thing as bop music, but there's
> such a thing as progress.' – Coleman Hawkins

Although jazz's sepia, acetates, and lacquers
have dipped the black into silver nitrate,
and are faded little faders, they inflate like lungs.

The pink lung, with its tortoiseshell shellac
appears to bulge, and its inseam exhales
purity, and inhales spoonfuls of tempo.

Purity in jazz, sir, is thwarted and unutilized.
Two hundred years of minstrels, snapping
their red suspenders, corrode and oxidize the air.

Mr. Tambo: *What kind of a girl was she?*
Zip: She was *highly polished; yes, indeed. Her fadder was a varnish-maker...*
You see, that rubber pork chop became something.

Bechet's *Shim-Me-Sha-Wabble*, from its mold
has been heated and mounted face-to-face with a hinge
so that the machine opens up facing you.

It is not lieder or intermezzo, frozen like trout
beneath the flux and ratamacuing of ice. It is not alpine:
Eingeschlafen auf der Lauer / Oben ist der alte Ritter...

Through the cracked photos, breaking into creosote,
superlatives douse the monoliths: 'virtuoso,' 'genius.'
But there is a siphoning-off of licking pink jam from the knife:

Negativities: the integrated bands, for example, of alcoholics,
benzedrine-heads, and junkies, or the deranged catastrophe
of Buddy Bolden feeding his hand to a ceiling fan,

or the wicks saturated with amphetamines,
or Buddy Rich telling the trumpet section of 'fuckfaces'
that he'd plink them every seven bars like a neutered werewolf.

When Coleman Hawkins stood half-nude like a mango
in Friedlander's photo (1956) with his curved man-breasts
sweating from *It May Not Be True*, he appears modern.

He is not a manqué nostalgic, an item, logistical.
He – lung of aerate, propulsive tub, urgently pumping ninths –
is the living demonifuge, ripping through a blanket of vanilla radio.

Racial animus, intractable sources, faded scriptures,
the pinstripes of the Storyville mudheads, midwives,
and the peach tintypes fitted into ladies' brooches

are not jazz. This strategy does not puff the uvula's
blowpipe or bring an axe to the Vanguard.
Rather, it shufflebucks, pantomimes, and dabs slop with a hankie.

Meanwhile, as the onyx rattlesnake of the century
slid by 1960, the year the fedora went up the flue,
jazz, too, opened like a fire in a woman's ceremony – it did not end.

Ayler had yet to drag the black river into rivulets of need.
Unkempt skinny dips, red vinyl seats of the Southern buses,
and the vinegar cloud of the trees' harpsichords were made,

too, of a jazz. As the bus ate the road's tape measure,
the ballrooms closed, the Hickory House sewed
52nd Street into a flytrap enmeshed with liquid static.

65

The green river you ignore is realized by the black river
growing wings beneath the shoulder blades of the hatchling: –
Coleman Hawkins who morphs with alular quills into a hawk.

Dark patagial marks on underwings, present on all ages and races,
conjured shadows beyond the last section of the long film.
You're afraid of listening to this lady? He, too, with parade float head,

eyes like flashing lindyhoppers, lunging with the lumpy fabric
of the past, pushing his gauge, a deuce of blips, bloodstream
lush as a viper, is more righteous than scumpteen codification.

In closing sir, the reed was always remoistened while you were in the booth,
cutting the montage sequence. But the pink sequins of Bessie Smith,
quenched with yielding limelight, disappear into dust like eighth notes.

My button ejects and the tongue spits out the disk's rainbow.

The Conversation: a tape, a plastic wall, a bug, a saxophone

Abstract

I offer a discussion of an obscure film made more than 30 years ago, a film that has invisible hinges: on one side of the door *The Conversation* is a film about audio surveillance, audio recording, the private moments in public spaces that are heard and overheard. On the other side, it is about jazz, an amateur artist whose impulses struggle against his ordered, ordinary life. The film is about cameras, microphones, listening, and losing ground. It is about a person who salvages the moments of expression he has been desperate to repress.

Invader of Privacy

Francis Ford Coppola's 1974 film *The Conversation* uses jazz to examine Gene Hackman with his pants off (private) and Gene Hackman with a microphone scope (public), the idea of audio and video surveillance, and Harry Caul's (Gene Hackman) obsessive personality. The film offers a nuanced suggestion that jazz – particularly the tenor saxophone – is one of only two ways into Caul's isolated, paranoiac personality. The other is Catholicism, the methodical, ritualistic facets of which, like jazz, accentuate Caul's psychological states. Caul plays over recordings until the psychological and physical barriers or shells that he has constructed to protect himself have been dismantled; he improvises freely amid the ruins of his destroyed apartment.

In fact, if you destroy your apartment, tearing the floorboards like a hammer claw, your plastic Madonna in a shard, and your vinyl strap around your neck like a rubber halo, where do you go, and what sound – the lunatic antique green – pumps from the horn like the antlers of Moses?

Voice Judgments

The Conversation uses repetition to voice judgments about wiretapping, ethics, responsibility (privacy's many arms), and musical expression: each of these themes is the pearl key of understanding – how information maintains power, and how belief is a mist over a town called perception. Walter Murch's careful editing of the images and sound of a single repetitive conversation allow the filmmakers to unusually combine elements of a Hitchcockian thriller with a study of a character's single perspective. Because the viewer is only permitted to know what Caul knows, when he knows it, we are as surprised as he is when his recording reveals nuanced information about the conversation he has recorded. The film is as careful a study of Harry Caul as Caul is an expert at audio surveillance. The film suggests that Caul, like many of the ethically flexible, yet banal people involved in surveillance of peoples' private lives, is a pathetic and chilling character. *The Conversation* uses music in the narrative (Diegetic) and music Caul can't hear (Extradiegetic) to juxtapose private desire and public knowledge.

A speaker or a microphone, with the dense black mesh or molded black foam, hears all. It discriminates not, and looks straight unblinking, from the fog, into the cloud. Cast among the spires, there are raised voices and silenced voices. There is a wind, a vineyard, an amen, names, same nomenclature, the nature of conversation.

Extras

Coppola has said that he was attracted to the jazz musician because the saxophone approximates the human voice and offers a glimpse into a lonely soul experiencing angst. *The Conversation* begins with a shot of San Francisco's Union Square. An electronic telephoto lens tracks Caul being followed by a mime (Robert Shields). The mime, a mimicking silent observer, is a metaphorical double for Caul, who surreptitiously records others while revealing little or nothing of himself. He moves around to a band playing Hughie Cannon's 'Bill Bailey (Won't You Please Come Home)?' which is where we see the first saxophone of the film. 'All I want is a nice, fat recording', Caul claims, but a claim that's a lie or self-deception; he actually begins to care deeply about what his subjects are talking about.

The liar is seeking liars, for the private rhubarb salted-down in a big pot of boiled water. Those who are captured in the dark pupil of the lens are also students of a larger lesson: that raw echo bouncing off the sky is your own conscience and you can't go home again. The place is destroyed, the stuffing has been removed from the cushions. The keyhole has been cracked with Freon and the pilot light has been left on.

Piano Theme

The theme of the film's soundtrack, composed for solo piano by David Shire, begins when Ann (Cindy Williams) sees a homeless man on a park bench and says: 'I always think... that he was once somebody's baby boy and he had a mother and father who loved him and now there he is half-dead on a park bench.' Her words and the piano theme are repeated throughout the film.

Coppola's idea for the film was to alter the dramatic situation of a functionary dropping off a tape in an office in exchange for an envelope of money. Instead of following people being recorded, the film follows the man doing the recording, and enters his private life. When Caul goes home, he opens multiple locks and turns off an alarm. Startled to discover his landlady has left him a bottle of wine for his birthday, Caul calls her to find out how she infiltrated his security systems. Here the camera is static. Rather than following Hackman as he moves on and off screen, the camera itself becomes the object of surveillance. The camera is a dead or passive observer, like Caul and the homeless man on the bench; only after 'realizing' that Hackman isn't returning to the frame

69

does the lens follow him to further eavesdrop, panning left to the sofa, behind which a building across from Caul's is being demolished. The building is another symbol of a structure being destroyed, revealing the space or silence within.

What would a camera see if nothing was ever lost? Simone Weil says to erase the past is, perhaps, the greatest of all crimes. If no one was ever missing, would the camera matter? What if what was captured within Nadar's frame, within Bellocq's frame, within Francis Wolff's frame, was not the musician, dusty from the bench, but the canyon's echo spinning from oval to circle? You never miss your water till your reed gets dry.

At these moments, the camera offers one of the few looks into Caul's world. Even the name Caul implies a kind of shell, like the semi-transparent plastic raincoat he wears regardless of the weather. Caul creates innumerable barriers to prevent those around him from getting close to him. Saxophone is a way to escape; to be his truer self.

Sax Practice
Caul's music does not use repetition: he practices his saxophone; the music he plays is heard. He does not hear Shire's piano theme. A singular moment of access to Caul's denial; the sax breaks through the layers of deception he has maintained. So deliberate are these layers that Caul lies to his girlfriend, Amy Fredericks (Teri Garr), by telling her he's 42 rather than 44. Although he pays her rent and visits her occasionally, their relationship is strongly one-sided: she yearns for closeness and even superficial information about his life, but he visibly becomes uncomfortable and leaves when she asks too many questions. 'I don't have any secrets,' he tells her when she says, 'I'm your secret' and that he has a 'special way of opening the door'. This scene in which Amy tries to break through Caul's layers and Caul's retreat is punctured by his surprising explanation of his job: 'I'm

a kind of a musician', followed again by the piano theme. Amy presumably has a life outside of Caul's occasional visit, but that life is hidden. Her bicycle, hanging on the wall, is covered in a transparent plastic sheet ('a caul'). Like his raincoat, the plastic seems to imply a semi-porous way for Amy to leave Caul's orbit. When she breaks up with him he has no reaction: his mind wanders to Ann and Mark (Frederic Forrest), the young couple he recorded.

Emerson speaks of the currents of a transparent eyeball. A transparent wall and a transparent raincoat make Teri Garr sad. A viol frozen in stone, and the pale medusa twisting in her German bones.

Mirrored Glass
Although the scene with Amy suggests that Caul's secrecy will alienate those around him, *The Conversation* examines surveillance as a joke, a gag, mocking, behind the silver glass. For example, as Caul and Stan (John Cazale) record the couple at the start of the film, two women apply lipstick in Caul's van's mirrored windows. Believing they're actual mirrors and not two-way mirrors / windows, they are unaware Stan is photographing them. When Caul visits the Director's (Robert Duvall, uncredited) office, the Director's Assistant Martin Stett (Harrison Ford) has a telescope and later sees both Mark and Ann in their office. When Caul is alone with Ann in the elevator, she is unaware that he knows anything about her. His memory repeats: 'Who started this conversation anyhow?' The stylus is stuck inside the groove.

If you repeat something enough, you become a tiny figure stacked in a glass shape; 'the little hands are mine'; it is a cell that you alone suffer from. What about the toy that is pink marble, male-female, a little puddle of precious liquids, the saliva from a lamb chop that rests on the floor, enclosed in a transparent bag?

Now Playing

Memory loops, redactions, amnesiac garbles, and interruptions of repetitions are the aural moments that consume Caul, and, by extension, viewers, who, observing the conversation, must consider their own complicity in violating privacy. For example, during the repeated loop of the mime following the couple, the mime's silent participation (unnoticed by the audio equipment built by Caul himself) is echoed by Ann's comment, 'I think he's (the Director) been recording my telephone'. Thus, the modes of private confession and public hearing are affirmed and exposed. Likewise, when Caul, a practicing Roman Catholic, visits confession, one of the oldest forms of surveillance, he confronts the hidden truth that his work may have lead to three homicides. Caul's religiosity is based on guilt and shame rather than faith. The priest (Richard Hackman, Gene's brother) is barely visible behind an opaque lattice screen. Religion and jazz – the only ways Caul allows his personal life to crack the façade. His saxophone and a plastic Madonna are the only items in his apartment that differentiate it from a motel room. He is fanatically determined to keep others out of his apartment (even though the landlady and presumably a rival wiretapper get in). This impulse is an attempt to soothe his guilt, mask his vulnerabilities, and maintain his sealed exterior. The transparent sheet in Caul's workshop, another caul, is a symbol of this sealed concealment.

Through a sexual connection, the couple moves, like a blue fox, sliding across each other, but then *le désir de plaire* pushes the tail of one into (or below) the opening. I can't remember her name, but the ceiling was a lovely cobalt blue. Even further from the others, she turns in a way – economical – that way of the sea floor invading the sky, and the sky answers somehow by raining.

No Name, No Address

Anonymity, and its violation of permeable barriers, are

endlessly examined by *The Conversation*. Coppola filmed the wiretappers' convention at an actual wiretappers' convention in Washington, D.C. Caul sees the Assistant Director on a camera's monitor and later confronts him in a mirrored hallway; a man carrying a saxophone passes in front of Caul and Stett. At the convention, William P. Moran (Allen Garfield), Caul's East Coast rival, secretly bugs Caul with a recording pen. After arguing with Caul about the legitimacy of being interested in the conversation, Stan begins working for Moran, and Caul discovers from a phone operator that he will likely never hear from Amy again.

The recording plays during Caul's reluctant sexual encounter with Moran's assistant, Meredith (Elizabeth MacRae) when he confesses: 'I have to destroy the tapes'. Moran is in awe of Caul's accomplishments, but he is a superior bugger in other ways, and has access to Caul's workshop of homemade equipment. However, the only way Moran can gain access to the secret tapes is by enlisting Meredith to steal them. Coppola has said that lovers who gain confidence in each other participate in one of the oldest modes of confession and surveillance.

Nixon was one of those guys from Yorba Linda nicknamed 'Dick' who hated reds, pinks, or even mauves. Increasingly paranoid, he refused to work on divorce cases because he was embarrassed by women's sexual misconduct, and as a Quaker, he espoused 'nonviolence.' Jack Paar shows Nixon playing a piano concerto, with a lonely, fragile-as-glass technique.

Dreamscape
Caul has a dream, intended to be the final sequence of the film, in which he addresses Ann in a foggy landscape. He tells Ann that after a childhood illness and partial paralysis, 'I was disappointed I survived...but I'm not afraid of death'. When Caul wakes up the next morning, he realizes that Meredith has stolen the tapes and given them to the Director.

Martin Stett tells Caul that he must have the tapes because Caul knows how dangerous they are. He has no idea what Stett is talking about until he discovers Mark's sentence, 'He'd kill us if he got the chance', inaudibly hidden behind some bongos. Frederic Forrest gives two slightly different readings of this line, repeated at various times during the film: one with the emphasis on *kill* and the other with the emphasis on *us*. Here, *The Conversation* pays its greatest homage to *Blow-Up*, in which a seemingly innocuous photograph shows the evidence of a murder – but only when it is enlarged. Caul discovers the couple may be murdered (he actually has this detail backwards) when he somehow omits the foreground noise that is obscuring it. *Blow-Up*'s final scene, where some mimes play tennis with an invisible ball, is replayed in Caul's slightly different hearing of the word 'us,' which has been hidden from the audience until Caul's paranoia is the puff pastry swirling with hot oven air.

The most revolting thing about a peach is the human-like fur. You bite it as if you are making love to your ex-lover, who now hates you, but you believe that after the funeral it is better to make a connection, a human one, rather than suffer alone. The juicy flesh and the solid, wrinkled pit of shame.

Blood
Obscurity and anonymity are Caul's métier: he tells Amy and Stett that he doesn't have a home telephone. His own ignorance shocks him him when he sees Ann's photo in the Director's office. Caul decides to find out what is happening in Room 337, where Mark and Ann have murdered the Director. The scene of Caul under the sink next to the toilet is a visual pun on the term 'plumbers,' the name for the Watergate wiretappers. Caul experiences his dissociation from reality as a discussion of Nixon's State of the Union address plays on the television. The blood rushing from the

toilet (Caul's guilt?) is an allusion to terror and appliances in *Psycho*. Is the blood real or merely in Caul's mind? In fact, the difference is meaningless if Caul, supposedly a genius, is actually bad at his job. When Caul sees Ann in the back of the Mercedes 600 limousine and the Director's corpse wrapped in a transparent plastic sheet he realizes his mistake. Martin Stett, Ann, and Mark are now aware that Caul is aware of them and knows they murdered the Director. The audio surveillance expert is now himself the target of audio surveillance.

We say blood, but we mean 'family.' We say machine, but we mean 'automatic.' What is more horrifying than being in someone's home — a dinner party, a first date — and the toilet water keeps coming up and up? You stand there, panicked, sweaty. There is nothing to do but feel your own mistakes bubbling like a red-brown nightmare.

Transmitter, Foil, Radio, Satellite, Binary
Caul begins scanning his rooms for a bug and totally destroys his apartment. The physical deterioration of Caul's environment matches his psychological descent. Where is the bug hidden? Caul believes it is hidden inside his plastic Madonna, but when he destroys it, he discovers nothing. Coppola said he does not know where the bug was hidden, and the viewer never finds out if there was a bug at all. But when Coppola suggests that perhaps it is attached to Caul's saxophone strap, which he never removes, it raises the possibility that Caul's attachment to jazz (literally and figuratively) allows others to penetrate his façade.
Much of the information in jazz is visual as well as aural. Why do we see and hear Caul as a jazz figure? *The Conversation* engages and 'worries' the concept of Caul as musician and his audio surveillance expertise in multiple ways: The musician as amateur, who hears the background music even as he tries to break free from it; Caul is only able to break free when he is unable to locate the bug,

yet knows he is being 'heard'; The musician as flâneur, who strolls around Union Square (and tells Amy he is an itinerant musician) whil a mime silently mimics him; each is a mimetic audio observer trying to piece together a composite portrait of those observed; The musician as someone with faith, who believes in the predetermined chord changes, and applies his imaginative persona around them; Caul is presumably only 'himself' during his moments of expression in the confessional and during his improvisations; The musician as Heraclitus, who never plays the same song the same way twice; when Caul first hears Mark say 'He'd *kill* us if he got the chance' and later say 'He'd kill *us* if he got the chance' his understanding and his psychological state lets him hear the line differently; The musician as a tableaux of psychic space, who allows the material of his private life to enter a public space; Caul's burgeoning responsibility toward his craft affects the quality of his craft because he is unwilling to give the recording to anyone but the Director; The musician as listener, who interprets the information from his audio surveillance of other sounds (e.g. bass, drums); Caul maintains the stance of a dispassionate observer, but he is only actually able to hear what they're saying when he becomes emotionally involved in his recording; The musician as jazzographer, or as producer of the text; Mark and Ann, as players in their own production create the complete recording, which is spliced from three incomplete recordings; they believe they are illicitly eluding the recording, and even offer fake laughter to disrupt it; Caul is able to recreate the recording from its pieces, and acts in accordance with hermeneutics, or renewal through interpellation and interpretation; The musician as a samurai, feeling his own mortality; when Caul becomes emotionally obsessed with the recording he privileges its interpretation even at the expense of his own life, and this privilege occurs in tandem with his jazz expression; The musician as producer of mood, texture, and a nonverbal plot; *The Conversation* and *Blow-Up* are both attempts at the multiple perspectives achieved when repetition is used as a device to invade private moments. The shotgun microphone with a sight, for example, that Caul's team uses to obtain the recordings, allows the constant repetition of the same fragments of the conversation to clarify ideas in elastic time. Multiple valences or reactions occur to both Caul and the viewer of the film as the debris of the conversation are endlessly reexamined (e.g. 'Who started this conversation, anyhow?').

Like the magic mirror maze in Orson Welles's *The Lady from Shanghai* (1947), also filmed in San Francisco, Caul is unmade by the repetitive nature of his obsessive focus on the repeated recording. Multiple cameras and microphones recorded the conversation between Cindy Williams and Frederic Forrest in real time, amid a real crowd in Union Square, in the middle of the day. Like Rita Hayworth shooting multiple reflections, Coppola and Murch decided to with difficulty replicate the recording of the conversation in *The Conversation*. The experience, then, of diegetic and extradiegetic sound, are bound and mixed in odd ways. Murch reveals that Williams and Forrest later rerecorded the exact dialogue with exact intonations and gestures in a quieter location so that the filmmakers would not have to act as their own Harry Cauls, forced to splice together inaudible moments.

Jazz Death?

If jazz is about audio moments, then Caul successfully breaks free of his shells within shells after he is bugged and cannot resolve where the bug is located. However, Caul is an obsessive-compulsive and paranoiac personality who begins to question his responsibility – will his recordings be used to plot a murder? He relies on the saxophone to serve as his ersatz voice. Being a musician is his fantasy – as he reveals to his mistress Amy; his access to a world of sound allows him first to document, then to penetrate the conversation that initially appears valueless. Caul becomes aware that despite his efforts to prevent a murder, his recording neither prevents nor makes possible the Director's killing. He has become attuned to recording others, so when he is the one recorded, he resigns himself to playing the jazz music without accompaniment, as if to accept his own fate as producer of and listener to sound.

In a vault, on the bracketed, machined metal shelf, there is a reel-to-reel. It's got a paper box and a faded label. 'Memories,' the masking tape peels off, and beneath that another scrawl in magic marker: 'Remember,' but that, too, is crossed-out. Redacted photos show a red X over his head, but in the re-telling of it, it's the brother and not me who pushes the other into the corner. Okay, but who has the scar?

The Seventies
The Conversation remains one of the most important films of its decade, and Coppola has said it was his favorite of all his films. It successfully navigates peoples' uneasy feelings about private conversations and public access to them, an increasingly topical idea in the age of electronic repetition of binary code, blogging, Twitter, and social networking. The obsessive nature of its 'hero' and the camera eye itself are methods by which the audience is also implicated in their voyeuristic knowledge of private talk. Caul's contradictory feelings of impotence and omnipotence masterfully exploited by Hackman shows the conflict of his exploitation by both Duvall's Director and Coppola as Director: perhaps Caul is more passive than he realizes. This film uses jazz as a strategy to expand its character study, rather than as a subject matter, and in doing so expands the function of jazz as a metaphorical language.

Mountainous Black Garden

> 'What good is intelligence if you cannot discover
> a useful melancholy?'
> – Akutagawa Ryonosuke

Reading grapefruit, prey, and fake grief.
Put on 'Fleurette Africaine' and her arm

Drapes onto steel fibers along nerves.
Her love fills the zinc bottle of its own body.

Peel me a woody bass, wick the piano away
From the sweet peak of Duke's pomade.

Black can be quiet and contain the whole thing.
What is apart and not hard and hard and not apart?

Apotheosis of Sonny Clark

First, tar's vinegar warmth, euphoria & nodding off.
Followed by Automat cheeseburgers and vanilla milkshake.

The only black kid in the school picture,
Faraway swim look in the thread of his eye.

Japanese love *Cool Struttin'* –
White legs, black A-line, Fifth Avenue.

As demons douse metallic nodules
A stylus pins Cole Porter in a Pullman quarter.

What seems like a right hand with blue tabulae
Is actually Sonny Clark waking up from his vomit

When he sees what he's leaving behind
Only the right chord is perfect labor

Everything with Sonny Clark is weakness.
He's a city and a forest infolded quill

Tranquilized with black lung and tar black,
The most aristocratic color of all.

Theme for Maxine

Blow powdered color thru a straw.
From the cave's vantage, feel the trestles and palms.

Be the 'flash lab' – see a ball slow above the plate.
Be the 'flesh lab', too – the cream of your neck, the portion near the ear.

Use your stylus; have no direct hand contact.
Recall that utopia literally means 'not a place.'

Punishment: Write 'I will not write this poem'
1,000 times on a wall. Then hinge that wall, or singe it...

I think of Maxine H. sometimes...her inky bob,
Ramones T, and negative definitions.

We would ride her blue Toyota behind the dunes.
Clear-cell cancer killed her years ago.

She would take my hand in the mid-grade mall
We saw our liquid happiness rising through bodies.

Trombone Magic

'the exigencies of an interval'
– Igor Stravinsky

Ory's gooey nasty bone style,
with its slurs, gloss, and muskrat dust
reveals a muskrat, an aquatic rodent, and its fur,

all Louisiana industry before Ory
relocated to Los Angeles. Thoreau described
their nests not as *things*, but as dwellings,

the border of habitat & town. The theme
beneath the soli on 'Dropping Shucks' with
corn shucks and their outside maize used

for toilet paper. Lil Hardin's feelings
of revenge during their divorce, dropping
them on Louis's head. The raw umber of marrow,

A bone, facing backwards on a horse-drawn
cart when the sun sets there is naught to do
I saw you with your sweet man last night
And I know you wasn't true.

Final Performance

for David S. Ware (1949-2012) and
for Stefan Zweig (1881-1942)

'The outcasts of the world...love with a fanatical,
a baleful, a *black* love.' – Stefan Zweig

Let's just saw ourselves in half
and call it a night.
It's easy to seep fifteen grains
as the barbital's green bandages sprawl
out and out with its sinews,
with its black oak ripening.

Step over the duff on the forest floor.
The rings supply the breath,
which is being furze-brushed and trammeled.
The last night the Quartet played
a skunk rolled down and ruptured its larynx.
The stump thought the skunk stunk.

But sifting the Veronal in his drink like hash,
Zweig felt the ouzelo, throstleo, cushato, culvero,
and syrupo on his wing.

Benjamin Franklin said nine men in ten
are chronic suicides, but for Zweig
the curvature of the Earth was too dark,
with its river orchestras and plumy effluvia.

One way is to slip into the tub
like a pearl in wine and phosphenes
stoke you like a virgule with quartz dust.
Another is to pity yourself into.

As the Quartet ended, each pearled key quit,
each string quieted. Like a palindrome,
the mustachioed Zweig shrunk into his fat baby self,
and devolved into a baby –
Doc, note, I dissent. A fast never prevents fatness. I diet on cod.

I heard the band play a dirge,
with its edge, and could assuage each, outdistanced.
Who here has not considered diving
like a species of rail. Flightless marsh, who will sink today?

Nothing affects us more than the unlived lives
of our parents. The slender twigs
and sugary gems fall on the moist ground.

But between the heart and head
the Quartet's barbiturate
floated in the red mukula air.
The plum pudding air is red with raining heat,
in droplets deep in the interior.

This heart is dried on hooks, then the massive,
steamed, effectively black
suet is in a drum. In its room, four rooms, actually...
is an *ecstasis* of the yellow flesh.
In a drum is a room, and on the moor
is a murder. Remain there drinking rum
as the broom leaves the dust alone.
More for the roost till the toxins enter
and we rest.
Though there are no plums in it,
there are cloves and candied citron.
Zweig called it 'the eternal rhythm
of the onward and onward'
though his subject, like that of the Quartet,
was human limitation.

This romantic fruit with its amber flesh
and multiple pollenizers, should be cooled for 900 hours:
Earliqueen, Murietta, Crimson Glo, and Royal Zee...
when these maroon hearts are
bitten, know the juice and flowing nubiana.

Because Zweig and Lotte thanked
the people of Brazil, and died,
the last droplet
'stilled the paroxysm of sobs.'
A red light on a red van took them down.
The four wheels
like cradled rhododendrons.
The uncontaminated ship slows
and between its pivots, like a seed,
she purls into the sea.

Purplish-blue, the great caravanserai
wheedle through the sand;
Zweig in his bed with Lotte,
as their hands crisscross in surging underbelly.

Blame Zweig's defection
on the 'climacteric'
but the indelible vortex of the fruit
and its upholstery touches like a shadow.
Half of us seeping limestone, brass,
the eve of Singapore falling to killers.
What is the price, for incursion,
even as the unicorn's liver bubbles like a dungeon?

We're sawed in, like a seesaw,
with laughter, but in the gut, here where Zweig
is pointing, is a gutter ball.
The ordure piles in the mouths
of the ones we call Father.

I heard a quarter of a musician
and did not hear a third of border's scorn.
Here and there is
a daughter, swaying like a saw,
with resin and paint. The saw, framed in lime,
seemed to tout a court. Then, in halves,
this monkey with its larder
was a mock hanging.

Dust into dust and plum into summer
like a brood the four stood.
One daughter then said to the other:
I am unsure of anything
but the endless interminable chatter
of the mind.

All These Things Are Not Without Their Meanings

Within you a red box with a needle.
It lands and plays a song.
The songs shimmer like moonlit bones
full with defective, long stories.

A train rolls by the sea in Connecticut
but your needle hardens like a brick
in a bag in a box in the sea.

To feel without the object of desire
is to cluster around feeling.

If you dragged me to a green sofa
and reclined upon me on it, an image
in my leaden glass,
would I, like the shape
of a wing unfurl and fly
into you burning lists of addresses
and grateful for every syllable of your
rising skin? Would the night lengthen,
inside-out as my chest unlocks revealing
three lesser chests, as you arrive in a newly painted place,
light as an envelope, fallen in a black room?

My final letter is in the mailbox and I hear it thud
the bottom, like something you should not have overheard
your parents talking about.

Lesser chests:

1. of a child, foaming and constructed like a hallway
with its pink doors, holes and shushlings.

2. of the new day, the master of a whole world,
a bag full of walnuts, lemons, and licorice.

3. of now. When I wake,
you are there, in woolen vagaries and scarlet angels.

For a Depressed Woman

What happened to the darkness of the grape of the harness?
What happened to break in the steeple of the alarmist?

There is a chalk on the wall, schist of Morningside.
Even scarlet and rib-like silver in a cube.

You're asleep in all your clothes and the baby, too, sleeps.
Something sucks the liquid from the bottom of an empty glass.

Kneading and dryflexing, these heavy airs make their way
To the harp-like sea...a heaving sour rind still alive in me.

There is a woman here, where she be, a canary in a cavern
Yellow among the windsongs, useable rain, and inmost granite.

Disassembled Parts of a Bass Clarinet

I.

Aerophone. Overblow. Grenadilla. Cylindrical bore.
Sassafras. Contrabass. Orange tiger. Roar.

Harry Carney. Half-hole. *Bitches Brew*. Resin.
Cousin Mary. Eric Dolphy. Grapefruit stew. Rosin.

Neither a dry sound, nor the white ricepaper mask,
But, swallowing the moon, the notes drink like grapes.

The Newark photographer says that when he was a kid,
There were 12 or 13 movie theaters downtown.

Now, only a tiny porn theatre, a spit's distance from the Museum,
Shows octaves of skin. Part of the lip stretches behind the knee,

Smooth as a Mercury reissue, and the precipice, glistening
Like a roll's glaze, has been pushed up and down across

Sarah Vaughan's orgasmic 'Uh' noise at 2:35 in 'Body and Soul.'
The Dogon wear purple fringes, and their pearl millet

Sing vessels of donkeys bearing caryatids, like the sandstone
Bandiagara all rectilinear with masks secured by the teeth.

Four flutes roll off their center; the cake's filling, plastered
(Not a sigh, exactly longer) are references to barbecued peaches.

White and red altars catch clouds...is that what Braxton means?
I shook hands with Elvin Jones, and with Lawrence D. 'Butch' Morris.

The cavernous filaments of the downtown room, like a limb
Soaking in a barrel. An article said: The amount of female granaries

Is an indication of the amount of women living in the guinna.
Little Richard, with his nougat-like pomade, yelled the girl can't help it.

Coltrane, likewise, said whatever he'd say about Eric Dolphy
Would be understatement. Newark's dry-rot and magnesium

Flares show litter, and the bare branches of a maple. Some looters
Return with armfuls of candy, Kool-Aid, and water guns.

The late photo of Sarah Vaughan shows black triangles
Arranged like a batman villainess. Years ago her carefree loafers

And red Parisian mime stripes swung easy. The liner notes reveal
'That she could have succeeded in the classical field.'

Wayne Shorter would say 'What's happenin'?' and she'd say 'Newark,'
And that was enough, 'cause you know what Newark does to people.

Mel Torme reports that she got kind of huffy when he said 'operatic'
And then she said 'Do you mean jazz isn't legit?'

You might say that powders are being crushed in the mortar,
Where some of the purple splays like limbs, the embracing limbs.

For a while poetry did not interest me, with its flailing,
Corruption, boredom, obsequiousness, and general green color.

It was a cloak used for taunting by everyone, assholes all.
Flaubert thought the same thing about the bourgeoisie.

Nothing is ever the same as they said it was.
Blue lights of her hair, vertical, the gray pearls of her neck,

Delightful, to the place – better or worse – where eyes penetrate.
Bare forks, glitter swan glasses, hiding among the bushes.

Sort of feeling your way. Arbus said, *the hand is the cutting*
Edge of the mind. Flawed animals. Meat and buns and slaw.

She sort of lifted up her hips so the rims of the bones
Were elevated, a sort of handsclasp, of 'braided chestnut'

Then, a wordless moan, like the pink tent you traverse –
Rather than nonvocal to the bone, she pulled his shoulders

Forward, hovering. During rehearsal the wordless word was loosely
Creased, where the lowest part of the hip is hooked to the curve.

Roland Kirk's 'No Tonic Pres' has a double meaning:
The first note in the scale and the double gin Lester Young

Was drinking without quinine water, circumference of lemon
Like the brim of the hat, blooming into focus in Gjon Mili's film.

I gathered dry kindling on the snowy mountain slope,
White were the branches gathered in my hand.

Wood has dropped its pieces, with trees along the way,
Where the couple walks the trail inside the creamy sand.

The bassist said the action on the bass was high,
Vertically so, so that the elastic boom made for instant decay.

Threadgill says tubas can control the decay and attack.
Tubas blend with everything, whereas the bass doesn't blend.

Brass will cut through anything. You have to wait on the bass.
A tuba player, he says, can shut it down, 'cause it's wind.

The bass player said during a long jam, he never
Gets a break. The glass of Pepsi has water already

Dripping down the side of the glass. From the ice
Skating in the armful of warm air. A woman bends

To pat a multi-striped cat, liquid grey, who prances
Between the aisles, listless and revolting with mystery.

She loves the horrendous creature, whose eyes glow
Yellow like a vial of Pernod. Its tail upright

Plucking an e-minor because the story has become
More complicated than when we left the house.

Miles played in Tokyo and then Berlin, former
Scorched sectors alighted in the terror-bots' scopes.

In Tokyo on March 9, 1945 we (Americans) burned to death
100,000 people in a single night; men, women, children.

On July 14, 1964, Sam Rivers channeled T-Bone Walker
Among the velvet echoes at Kohseinenkin Hall.

The Dogon say that we should remember:
God has no external ears. She cups her hands.

Babies are like water flowers who devour
The cool leaves from the tubs of their eyes.

Our ways of living differ.

II.
Think of swagger's on-off switch.
Weldon Irvine said: Many of the young rappers

Got disconnected from a tradition of protest
And decided to rap about mayhem

In order to get paid. You can tell the political
Orientation of the bus driver by whether

He says 'Lenox Avenue' or 'Malcolm X
Boulevard' when he announces the stop.

The large blue and white wheels slap
The painted curb, covered with slush.

November '80. I walk to school
Not knowing how to play *with*.

I decided, not unlike John Gilmore
At Birdland 1956, to play *contra*.

We play against everything,
In the blaze of a hearth.

We got the concept. We got
The concept. We got conceptual.

I am on East 80th Street. The whir
Of pigeons have delicate lavender

Pockets around their eyes.
They ground themselves and a spring

Of city dust is a pillowy aplomb
Among the air's granules.

Of a city, and its puzzle pieces
Many-tongued, embraceable.

Two men are dancing in a bar.
It's 11:30 according to the wall's

Cold Aged 'Genesee Beer' clock.
They are dressed in 1980 styles: velour

And floppy, existential caps. The shadows
Of the men's bodies are cast

On the jukebox behind and their joy.
What do you know about the forgotten ones?

Try to understand the beautiful bodies,
Peeling paint, and upturned peaches

From a Marxist perspective. Why this city
Detritus, denotations and detonations?

Why the snail shell, uncomfortable water,
The caramel tone of Sarah Vaughan

And the air is punctuated by wings?
Instead of limbs, wings slice through

At 80 degrees, assaulting through
The sky's catapult, salted & polychrome.

I would like to be away from 1980
For a while, and see its chemical pinks

Dripping from the unfeeling dinosaur
Eye of the iridescent pigeons,

Another time, from above or below.
I will not take my father's footsteps.

A miner's helmet with its bulb
Peers through the tack and driftwood.

Around a wall, the light bounces
On a mirror with its white cotton.

You are encased in the city's
Steel tub. Washboard, scrap,

Empty grape drink bottle.
Frail, fall, literal. Burnished.

Do you feel the calm
Chewing the marrow

From the gains the city has made?

III.

A halved city moves
along the mouth of a canal.
You are living inside its corridors,
breathing the air shaft's smell
of a fishbone. Your limbs reach
across the threshold,
down the hallway of metal doors.
It is that multihued avenue
that comes at the park's edge
after a mollusk's snowdrift
away from the window mottled
jamb's coded, inconceivable rust,
the pigeons' peppery throats
blush like sorcerers bending the tab
rings of their cans, and all echoes.
It is not only pushers and gathering
places, storefront churches, crates of apples.
We should not be east of the park,
but no one knows we're here,
if it is the Paradise or the Omni
swaying along the velvet curtain of the sky.
Beyond the rooftops, I see

the families create a father's
day picnic out of a card table, boombox,
a ginger ale, boxes of chicken,
a dominoes game clamped to a dude's lecture.
I would run from the 125th Street station
down the sustained line of the sidewalk,
and wait for the elevator that stops
to raise its pulley and flywheel
and drop my trapezoid body,
and race to the apartment
to caress your hair,
or to let up or simply hold on.
It is a familiar curvature.
The place is a valley, the cathedral's east.
The same streets reach out
in the same places, to open
the same mirrored lobbies.
We arrive at the place
where the wife relaxes
and folds her legs on the floor
in conjecture
at all the sidewalks traversed.
She has me, a partner who knows
that her memories are bubbles,
that we see a farfetched capital lift,
and break through tenements
and wish like a creed,
we would travel along riffs and octaves,
to hear the doorbells and bird coos
or feel the extraordinary orange
of the Florida sun, a woman
clutching an orange pill bottle,
and we go along the snakelike namesakes
and the keratin hooves of the city
can always relieve us,
we have people sitting around
understanding the bubbles' gloss

anywhere the fragile, numb inheritances
answer the launching terrors
her axes and closet doors she remembers
we will burst them all along.

Sulfur Mustard

Syria since 2011

First the pineapple froth
In the lungs. A murmur
Beneath a layer of quartz means
Blood fangs suck uterus flesh
Into his darkling pit. Juniper ashes
Fume from a metal rod.

'Drive fast,' says the tour guide next.
'Along the 200 meter stretch
Ahead of you because there are snipers.'

Syria is someplace new. We are
Somewhere new, too, and we promise
The salmon-colored thing hanging
From the streetlight pumps breath,

Or pimps death. Take my hand, honey,
Along the spout of the thistle. This world

Was built by incompetents
Without knowing
If the future exists.

Embers of Smoldering Homes

It is a major war from
a manufacturing plant
near Ciudad Juárez, a concrete
dust smell from the maquiladoras
cools. There is a pool
of liquid forming
on the stone floor.
When Érika Gándara, the only
cop in Guadalupe Distrito Bravos
was killed the buzzards
were fucking in the wind.
See the brown ribs poking
through the side
of the hound, behind
the broken refrigerator.
The dog is looking for a guaco
leaf, or Saint Teresa.
She has not been seen
since two days before
Christmas. A painting
of the black Mary is wrapped
in plastic wrap, next to the rifle.
Who else is wrapped
in plastic, like drug baggies
or a piece of flesh: Praxédis, Leticia,
Esperanza, Hermila, Felicitas,
Lourdes, Elvira, Gabriela, Elsa Luz…
The body has been in the desert
for at least nine days.
A wire chicken coop,
a plaster wall, she vests herself
and waits for you like a hand
stripped of a moving world.
A hand stripped of a moving

world waits for you.
It snaps its fingers
on 2 and 4, a 'black snap'
or a sponginess encased
in desire. The fleshy leaves
of the agave bend a white
feather on a girl's brow.
The goatskin deflates
by the opening where,
lashed to itself, she pulls
back her flat breath,
her brittle and meager
clavicle unscrew the pain.
A niña's rose black edge
stumps the coroner
who says something is striking
me, my chrome raindrop,
my jacaranda, pouch of bone.
In Dublin, Ohio,
a sortie of jackals
split the scissors behind the mask
mouth and 'cut loose'
for a long needle-devouring night
into the rawhide axis
of dawn, of dung and ashes.
If the word Mexico means
'Place at the Center of the Moon'
then these fabric fireflies
and jutting hips are perfumed
honeyed vibrato moans
and the manic cartels
slice their own heads,
cancer-eaten, like a faceless jaw
snapping the desert moon.
We didn't meet in Mexico's
dark carbon, stretching palpitations
in black armor but a wooden

column of the archangel
who witnesses casually
the teporochos who eat genitals
and fuck watermelons.
When you take the last bus
to Piedras Negras a bullet
has struck the remaining tissue
not of livestock or bodyguard
but the moon's own leather aorta.

The Seventies

Corduroy collar, embroidered after-effects of olive teal.
Dawn of the decade: seventies – the event untied, of seven veins.

What do you do with the flame from the machine?
What does love mean when it rises like throat water?

Jungles are exploding with jellied gas, white meat of a sow.
Crayon velvet sharpens a person's eyeballs when the flesh comes.

Line dancers knot War's *The World Is A Ghetto* into a freshly minted up-do.
Malice, please take a seat, next to the butter dish's umbilical wallpaper.

Mary Ann Vecchio is here to place memory on a placard.
Bodies coated in white lime: a blowdryer under the neon moon.

Walnut interior, black wolf exterior: what does love do?
I am telling a lie: she had the exterior of grass: love does <u>what</u>?

Acknowledgments

Thank you to the editors of the following journals in which variations of these poems originally appeared:

Asheville Poetry Review 'Ken Burns'
Brilliant Corners 'Trombone Magic'
Cerise Press 'For a Depressed Woman' and 'The Seventies'
Critiphoria 'Italo Svevo' and 'Bruno Schulz'
CURA 'Sulfur Mustard'
Dorado 'Theme for Maxine'
Drunken Boat 'Albert Camus'
Electronic Poetry Review 'Frequency Hopping'
Fishousepoems 'Living on Nothing But Honey and Smoke' and 'Poem'
Guernica 'Treatise on Hank Mobley'
Hamilton Stone Review 'Black Swan'
The Inquisitive Eater 'Eating in Silence'
Mascara 'Encircle the pillow of grass' and 'Put On All the Lights'
Marsh Hawk Review 'Final Performance' and 'Violin (Larry Fine)'
Memorious 'Whale' and 'Disassembled Parts of a Bass Clarinet'
Mississippi Review 'Freud Knows' and 'Van Gogh Legerdemain'
Moment 'Ancestors Who Came to New York'
Pool 'All these things are not without their meanings'
Rethinking History 'The Conversation'
River City 'Poem' and 'Do You Believe We Shall Know Each Other When We Meet'
The Rumpus 'We Will Never Learn' and 'Embers of Smoldering Homes'
Salmagundi 'Franz Kafka – Serious About Your Safety'
Sea Change 'Sea'
Sou'wester 'Scott Joplin'
Worcester Review 'Apotheosis for Sonny Clark' and 'Mountainous Black Garden'

Grateful acknowledgement is made to the National Endowment for the Arts and the Massachusetts Cultural Council, through whose generous support this book was completed.

Thank you to Aaron Baker, CM Burroughs, Gabrielle Calvocoressi, Tina Chang, Oliver de la Paz, Saskia Hamilton, Adrian Matejka, Roger Mitchell, Simone Muench, Gregory Pardlo, Cecily Parks, Craig Morgan Teicher, Susan Thomas, Paul Zimmer, and Martha Zweig, who thoughtfully read early manuscripts. Thank you also to Todd Swift, Edwin Smet, and the entire Eyewear Team.

� EYEWEAR PUBLISHING